ANIMALS THAT BREAK THE RULES

Natasha Vizcarra

ROURKE'S SCHOOL to HOME CONNECTIONS
BEFORE AND DURING READING ACTIVITIES

Before Reading: *Building Background Knowledge and Vocabulary*

Building background knowledge can help children process new information and build upon what they already know. Before reading a book, it is important to tap into what children already know about the topic. This will help them develop their vocabulary and increase their reading comprehension.

Questions and Activities to Build Background Knowledge:

1. Look at the front cover of the book and read the title. What do you think this book will be about?
2. What do you already know about this topic?
3. Take a book walk and skim the pages. Look at the table of contents, photographs, captions, and bold words. Did these text features give you any information or predictions about what you will read in this book?

Vocabulary: *Vocabulary Is Key to Reading Comprehension*

Use the following directions to prompt a conversation about each word.
- Read the vocabulary words.
- What comes to mind when you see each word?
- What do you think each word means?

Vocabulary Words:
- ancestors
- biologists
- brooding
- chemosynthesis
- extinct
- marsupials
- monotremes
- prehistoric
- scat
- viviparous

During Reading: *Reading for Meaning and Understanding*

To achieve deep comprehension of a book, children are encouraged to use close reading strategies. During reading, it is important to have children stop and make connections. These connections result in deeper analysis and understanding of a book.

 ## Close Reading a Text

During reading, have children stop and talk about the following:
- Any confusing parts
- Any unknown words
- Text to text, text to self, text to world connections
- The main idea in each chapter or heading

Encourage children to use context clues to determine the meaning of any unknown words. These strategies will help children learn to analyze the text more thoroughly as they read.

When you are finished reading this book, turn to the next-to-last page for **Text-Dependent Questions** and an **Extension Activity**.

Table of Contents

What Is It? 4

Solar-Powered Animals 6

Reluctant Movers 10

Flightless Birds
& Walking Fish 12

Mammals That Lay Eggs
& Reptiles That Don't 16

Death-Defying Critters 22

Weird Poopers 26

A Quirky Advantage 28

Glossary 30

Index 31

Text-Dependent Questions 31

Extension Activity 31

About the Author 32

What Is It?

The colorful sea anemone confused early **biologists**, including the famous Greek philosopher Aristotle. The sea creature looked like a plant. So biologists named it after anemone flowers. But sea anemones eat little fish. So Aristotle classified it as *both* a plant and an animal. How can that be?

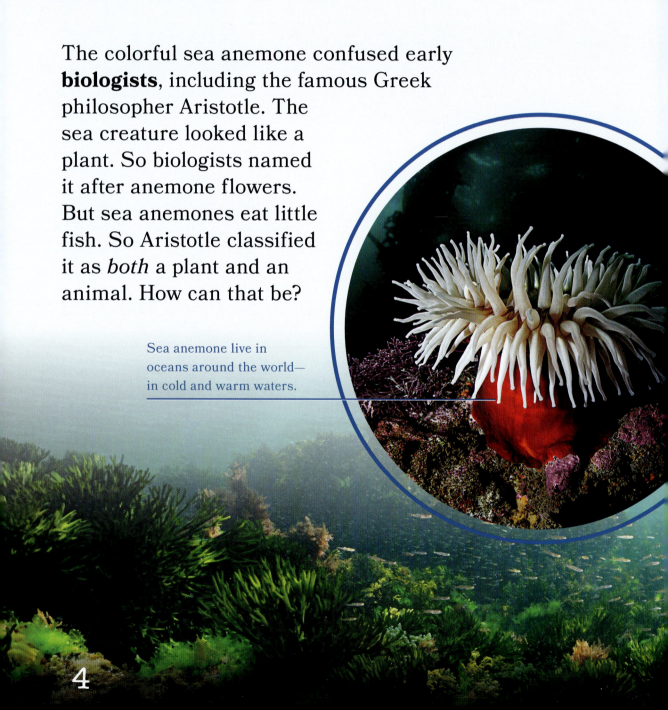

Sea anemone live in oceans around the world—in cold and warm waters.

Scientists eventually determined that the strange sea anemone is an animal. There are many other animals like this that boggle our minds. Some animals behave like plants. Some mammals lay eggs. Some fish would rather walk than swim. Get to know some of these wacky rulebreakers and why they are so quirky!

Sea anemone in tropical seas provide safe homes for clownfish. In return, clownfish chase away butterfly fish that like to munch on the sea anemone.

The hermit crab wears the sea anemone as a shield. The anemone's stinging tentacles scare away fish that want to snack on the crab.

Solar-Powered Animals

> **RULE:**
> ANIMALS EAT OTHER ORGANISMS TO SURVIVE.

Green Power

Photosynthesis is the process by which green plants make their own food using chlorophyll, carbon dioxide, and water when there is sunlight present. This sacoglossan sea slug acts like a plant and uses photosynthesis too!

The Costasiella kuroshimae sea slug is also called a "leaf sheep." Can you see why?

Biologists describe animals as living things that eat other living things to survive. They are different from plants which make their own food out of sunlight, water, and nutrients from soil. But what have we here? Animals that use photosynthesis the way plants do?

THE RULE BREAKERS:
PEA APHID, SACOGLOSSAN SEA SLUG, MARINE FLATWORM, SPOTTED SALAMANDER, AND ORIENTAL HORNET

Sea slugs munch on algae. Marine flatworms eat diatoms. Like plants, algae and diatoms can make their own food using photosynthesis. This is thanks to something called chloroplasts. When the sea slugs and flatworms eat them, the chloroplasts make energy in the animals' guts. Ta da! Free energy!

The Elysia chlorotica sea slug lives off the East Coast of the United States. It "recharges" the chloroplasts in its gut by sunbathing.

Three other critters take it a step further. The yellow-spotted salamander's eggs have algae in them. The algae perform photosynthesis and give oxygen and sugars to the baby salamanders. Then the algae receive the babies' poo as food.

Yellow-spotted salamanders only lay eggs in ponds that don't have fish in them. Otherwise, the fish would eat all the eggs.

The oriental hornet and the pea aphid don't need to steal chloroplasts. Their bodies capture sunlight and make electrons. These electrons move around inside their bodies and help produce energy.

Biologists are still trying to understand how these animals evolved to use photosynthesis. Many scientists hope they can use this information to make environment-friendly fuels or to help cures diseases.

Solar-Powered Hornets

Oriental hornets use the free energy to power their flight and digging. They live in holes in the ground.

Pea aphids favor pea, fava bean, and lentil plants. This is why vegetable gardeners don't like them.

Reluctant Movers

RULE:
ANIMALS MOVE ON THEIR OWN.

Sea anemones' stinging tentacles paralyze prey. This giant green anemone eats fish, crabs, and unlucky birds that fall into the water.

Animals move. They leap, pounce, swim, and fly on their own. That's one way biologists differentiate them from plants that are rooted to soil. But the sea anemone likes to stay in one place, like a plant. It's happy to just wait for food to drift by. The sea anemone anchors itself to rocks, pieces of wood, or the back of a crawling crab. It quickly wiggles away if something munches on it.

HESITANT RULE FOLLOWERS:
SEA ANEMONE, SPONGE, MUSSEL, AND BARNACLE

Other animals live anchored to a surface too. Sponges, coral, mussels, and barnacles attach themselves to rocks or the ocean floor. Barnacles even hitch rides on ships, sea turtles, and whales. These reluctant movers are all filter feeders. They pass water through their bodies to feed on plankton and nutrients.

Barnacles have attached themselves to sea turtles for more than 30 million years. Scientists found evidence of ancient barnacles on **extinct** sea turtle fossils in Germany.

Slow-Moving Critters

Young coral and some species of sponges, mussels, and barnacles can move slowly. For sponges, it comes at a cost. They leave bits of their bodies behind when they move.

11

Flightless Birds & Walking Fish

TAKAHĒ

RULES:
BIRDS FLY. FISH SWIM.

BIRDS THAT DIDN'T GET THE MEMO:
CASSOWARY, TAKAHĒ, KĀKĀPŌ, KIWI, OSTRICH, WEKA, STEAMER DUCK, AND PENGUIN

FISH THAT PRETEND:
RED-LIPPED BATFISH, SPOTTED HANDFISH, FROG FISH, FLYING GURNARD, AND WEST AFRICAN LUNGFISH

OVERACHIEVING FISH:
FLYING FISH

All birds have wings, so all birds fly, right? Not quite. The penguin and the weka swim instead.

The steamer duck, the cassowary, and the ostrich are too heavy to achieve lift off. The kākāpō's wings are too short for its body. The kiwi and the rare takahē run around like knee-high T. rexes.

These flightless birds all used to fly. Over hundreds of years, though, they lost the ability to fly because they didn't need to fly to survive.

Meanwhile, some fish can swim but would rather walk. Sort of. The red-lipped batfish, spotted handfish, frog fish, and flying gurnard waddle across the ocean floor. Water mostly holds them up. They don't need to swim to catch prey on the sea bottom. They just poke around for small fish, shrimp, or worms.

Wings For Flirting

Flying gurnards have wing-like fins. The males use them to attract females.

RED-LIPPED BATFISH

Kiwis can only be found in New Zealand. There are only about 70,000 kiwis left.

HAIRY FROG FISH

Living Fossil

The lungfish has gills and primitive lungs, allowing it to breathe air. It's a **prehistoric** animal that has been around for nearly 400 million years.

The West African lungfish doesn't just walk in water, it walks on land too. Its hind fins support its body and propel it forward. The lungfish feeds on fish, frogs, and snails. It also munches on tree roots and seeds.

West African lungfish like to burrow down into riverbeds.

And then there's the flying fish. It can swim, and it can also glide in the air! These fish aren't doing it for extra credit. They're doing it to survive! They learned how to launch themselves out of the water and glide on long webbed fins to escape predators.

Powerful Gliders

Flying fish can glide 164 feet (50 meters) at a time. When they ride ocean updrafts, they can glide as far as a quarter of a mile (400 meters)!

Flying fish are prey for larger fish like tuna, mackerel, and swordfish.

FLYING FISH

15

Mammals That Lay Eggs & Reptiles That Don't

RULES:
MAMMALS PRODUCE MILK AND GIVE BIRTH TO BABIES. REPTILES LAY EGGS.

MAMMAL OPPOSITION:
DUCK-BILLED PLATYPUS, WESTERN LONG-BEAKED ECHIDNA, EASTERN LONG-BEAKED ECHIDNA, SHORT-BEAKED ECHIDNA, AND SIR DAVID'S LONG-BEAKED ECHIDNA

REPTILES THAT REBEL:
DINOCEPHALOSAURUS, PLEISIOSAUR, BOA, VIPER, GARTER SNAKE, ANACONDA, RATTLESNAKE, SKINK, JACKSON'S CHAMELEON, AND **VIVIPAROUS** LIZARD

Mammals are animals that give birth to baby versions of themselves. For instance, female cats deliver kittens. Whales give birth to calves in the ocean. But did you know that there are mammals that lay eggs?

The duck-billed platypus, western long-beaked echidna, eastern long-beaked echidna, short-beaked echidna, and Sir David's long-beaked echidna are the only five species of egg-laying mammals in the world. They are called **monotremes** and can only be found in Australia and New Guinea.

Electrifying Skills

Platypuses and echidnas can sense electric fields. They use this extra sense to find prey.

Cutest Baby Name

Baby monotremes, like this wild baby echidna, are called "puggles."

So if monotremes lay eggs, why are they mammals? Monotremes share important traits with all mammals. They are vertebrates, meaning they have backbones. They are warm-blooded and have body hair or fur. They also breathe with lungs and produce milk to feed their young.

Scientists aren't sure why monotremes lay eggs. They are also surprised that they still exist.

Monotremes are ancient animals. There used to be so many more of them in Australia. When **marsupials** invaded Australia millions of years ago, many monotreme species became extinct.

Antarctic Ancestors

The oldest monotreme fossil is 130 million years old. Back then, southeastern Australia was within the Antarctic Circle. Monotremes used their electro-sensitive beak to find food during months of polar darkness.

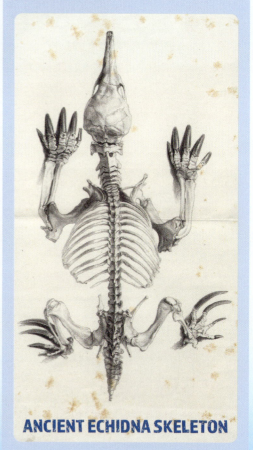

ANCIENT ECHIDNA SKELETON

When scientists examined the genes of today's monotremes, they found that the animals had swimming **ancestors**. In fact, the duck-billed platypus still lives part of its life in the water. Scientists think that monotremes are still around today because their ancestors escaped to where marsupials could not go—into the water.

Pouch Protection

Marsupials, such as wombats and kangaroos, keep their joeys in pouches for more than a year. This means they have to stay on land.

The duck-billed platypus is a shy creature. It spends its days feeding in the bottom of rivers and lakes, or resting in burrows.

Now let's meet reptiles that don't lay eggs like most of their slithery kind. More than 200 million years ago, dinosaurs laid gigantic eggs on land. But some long-necked marine reptiles said, "Nah!" Fossil records suggest the dinocephalosaurus and the plesiosaur gave birth to live young.

Most dinosaurs laid eggs. These troodontid eggs fossilized, and are on display at a Chinese museum.

Not Egg-cited About Eggs

The dinocephalosaurus is distantly related to modern-day crocodiles and birds that only lay eggs.

20

Today's boa constrictors, vipers, garter snakes, anacondas, and rattlesnakes don't lay eggs either. Neither do skinks, Jackson's chameleons, and viviparous lizards. They give birth to little versions of themselves, like mammals do. Scientists haven't agreed on why these reptiles opted out of egg-laying.

BOA CONSTRICTOR

JACKSON'S CHAMELEON

Why Not Both?

The three-toed skink lays eggs *and* gives birth to babies. It can also do both within a single litter of offspring!

21

Death-Defying Critters

RULE:
EXTREME ENVIRONMENTS KILL.

The wood frog is the only type of frog that lives north of the Arctic Circle.

Some critters can survive mind-boggling heat or cold. The wood frog survives the frigid Arctic tundra by freezing solid during the winter. It gets comfy in a pile of leaves. Its skin freezes and its eyes turn white. Then its heart stops. It essentially dies until it thaws and wakes up in the spring—nine months later!

THE SURVIVORS:

WOOD FROG, ARCTIC WOOLLY BEAR CATERPILLAR, GLACIER ICE WORM, POMPEII WORM, TUBE WORM, SCALE WORM, AND LIMPET

And then there's the Arctic woolly bear caterpillar. This finger-sized bug becomes a furry popsicle in the long, Arctic winters.

Another creepy crawly, the glacier ice worm, lives inside glaciers in North America. This worm is so adapted to the cold that it does not freeze. But expose it to temperatures just five degrees above freezing and it will disintegrate!

ARCTIC WOOLLY BEAR CATERPILLAR

23

Meanwhile, critters living on hydrothermal vents at the bottom of the sea survive extreme heat. The vents release sea water that can reach 175° Fahrenheit (79° Celsius). This heat can melt lead! That's just fine for Pompeii worms, tube worms, scale worms, and limpets. These animals live on chimney-like shapes rising out of the vents.

TUBE WORM

Underwater Hot Tubs

Hot bubbles are released from hydrothermal vents on the ocean floor. These vents are found on cracks in the Earth's crust or on underwater volcanoes.

CHEMOSYNTHESIS

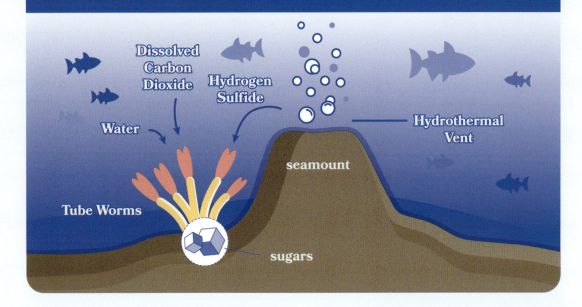

There isn't much food around these vents. Because it's so dark at the bottom of the ocean, sun-loving phytoplankton and algae don't live down here. These are two of the most basic foods in the ocean.

So how do these heat-loving marine animals survive down here? They depend on a process called **chemosynthesis**. Bacteria in their bodies convert chemicals from the vents into sugar. So all they have to do is hang out near these vents to be fed.

Weird Poopers

> **RULE:**
> POOP IS USUALLY ROUNDISH, DISCREETLY DROPPED, AND A THING TO GET RID OF

WOMBAT

Biologists study **scat** to learn about an animal's diet and territory. Some unusual poops have an interesting explanation.

The bare-nosed wombat drops cube-shaped poop. It turns out the last segment of this marsupial's intestines doesn't stretch out as much. This squeezes their poop into flat-sided cubes.

VULTURE

Vultures, storks, condors, gannets, and boobies repeatedly poop on their feet. Ick! Why would they do that? Studies show that the whitish poop helps cool the birds' bodies.

THE DEVIANTS:

BARE-NOSED WOMBAT, VULTURE, STORK, CONDOR, GANNET, BOOBY, AND PENGUIN

Penguins have projectile poop. Scientists think it's because **brooding** penguins want to keep poop away from their eggs.

Adelie penguins eat krill, and this turns their poop pink. They poop so much that Earth-observing satellites can see the color from space!

Fast-Moving Scat

Humboldt penguins launch fecal bombs at 5 miles per hour (8 kilometers per hour)! That's faster than American swimmer Michael Phelps' 100-meter freestyle speed at the 2008 Olympics. (His time was 47.51 seconds, or 4.71 miles per hour).

A gentoo penguin projectile poops. These penguins live along the coast of the Antarctic Peninsula.

27

A Quirky Advantage

Although quirky, rule-breaking animals are survivors. They have overcome challenges in their habitats. Their wacky and weird ways help them hunt for food faster and escape predators quicker. Breaking rules helps them protect their young, find mates, and find shelter.

STEAMER DUCK

MUSSELS

Humans have learned from these surprising animals. We have used these lessons to solve our own challenges.

Studying mussels inspired scientists to invent non-toxic glue that works underwater. The flying fish has inspired the robotic flying fish—a futuristic car that can swim and fly. Scientists studying sacoglossan sea slugs are hoping to find better ways to capture solar energy. We have a lot to learn from these fun and fascinating animals.

SACOGLOSSAN SEA SLUG

Glossary

ancestors (AN-ses-turs): members of a family who lived long ago

biologists (bye-AH-luh-jists): scientists who study living things

brooding (BROOD-ing): when a female bird sits on its eggs in a nest to incubate them

chemosynthesis (kee-moh-SIN-thuh-siss): the process by which microbes make food using chemicals as the energy source, typically in the absence of sunlight

extinct (ik-STINGKT): no longer found alive

marsupials (mahr-SOO-pee-uhlz): any of a large group of animals that includes the kangaroo, the koala, and the opossum

monotremes (MAH-noh-treemzh): egg-laying mammals

prehistoric (PREE-hi-stor-ik): belonging to a time before history was recorded in written form

scat (skat): wild animal poop

viviparous (vi-VI-puh-ruhs): producing live young instead of eggs from within the body

Index

Arctic woolly bear caterpillar 23
Aristotle 4
duck-billed platypus 16, 19
echidna(s) 16, 17, 18
Pompeii worm(s) 23, 24
red-lipped batfish 12, 13
sea anemone(s) 4, 5, 10, 11
solar energy 29
West African lungfish 12, 14
wood frog 22, 23

Text-Dependent Questions

1. Which Greek philosopher was baffled by the sea anemone?
2. Where can you find lungfish?
3. What are monotremes?
4. When does the sea anemone move?
5. How are marine flatworms like plants?

Extension Activity

The super cute duck-billed platypus is one of the most confusing critters in the world. It's an egg-laying, breast-feeding, duck-billed, web-footed, land and water-living, beaver-otter-looking, electric-field-sensing creature.

Draw a duck-billed platypus. On the left side, label traits that make it a mammal. On the right side, label traits that it shares with other kinds of animals. At the bottom, list traits that make it such a special critter.

About the Author

Natasha Vizcarra is a science writer and an award-winning children's book author. She likes cats, frogs, bees, wombats, sugar gliders, echidnas, and duck-billed platypuses. She lives in Colorado with her husband, Chris, and their three sometimes-rebellious cats. Learn more about Natasha and her writing at www.natashavizcarra.com.

© 2025 Rourke Educational Media

All rights reserved. No part of this book may be reproduced or utilized in any form or by any means, electronic or mechanical including photocopying, recording, or by any information storage and retrieval system without permission in writing from the publisher.

www.rourkebooks.com

PHOTO CREDITS: Cover: ©T33kid/Shutterstock, ©scooperdigital/Shutterstock, ©Vee Snijders/Shutterstock, ©WildMedia/Shutterstock, ©banjongseal324SS/Shutterstock, ©xpixel/Shutterstock, ©Martin Pelanek/Shutterstock; page 3: ©banjongseal324SS/Shutterstock, ©Eric Isselee/Shutterstock; page 4: ©Ethan Daniels/Shutterstock, ©Damsea/Shutterstock; pages 4–11: ©Damsea/Shutterstock; page 5: ©Antagain/Getty, ©Oxford Scientific/Getty; page 6: ©Pearawas Tangjitaurboon/Shutterstock, ©xlchen/Shutterstock; page 7: ©Namenam15/Shutterstock; page 8: ©WildMedia/Shutterstock; page 9: ©sujin vaipia/Shutterstock, ©nechaevkon/Shutterstock; page 10: ©Amanda Wayne/Shutterstock; page 11: ©Drew McArthur/Shutterstock, ©Ethan Daniels/Shutterstock; page 12: ©Wirestock Creators/Shutterstock; pages 12–23: ©xpixel/Shutterstock, ©banjongseal324SS/Shutterstock; page 13: ©Roberto Dani/Shutterstock, ©Ricardo_Dias/Shutterstock, ©Tamil Selvam/Shutterstock, ©Damsea/Shutterstock; page 14: ©Marzolino/Shutterstock, ©belizar/Shutterstock, ©SIR2480/Shutterstock; page 15: ©SIR2480/Shutterstock, ©Vladimir Turkenich/Shutterstock, ©vanessa da costa/Shutterstock, ©Daniel Huebner/Shutterstock; pages 16–19: ©Annalucia/Shutterstock; page 17: ©John Carnemolla, ©Ryan Hoi/Shutterstock; page 18: ©Penta Springs Limited / Alamy Stock Photo, ©hyotographics/Shutterstock; page 19: ©Martin Pelanek/Shutterstock, ©agymonion/Shutterstock; page 20: ©Gary Todd, ©22January/Shutterstock; page 21: ©22January/Shutterstock, Macronatura.es/Shutterstock, ©Eric Isselee/Shutterstock, ©Eric Isselee/Shutterstock; page 22: ©Yegor Larin/Shutterstock, ©Bruce R. Allen/Shutterstock,; page 23: ©Yegor Larin/Shutterstock, ©Kimberly Boyles/Shutterstock; page 24: ©Damsea/Shutterstock, ©22August/Shutterstock, ©bcampbell65/Shutterstock, ©Ethan Daniels/Shutterstock, ©Luca Vaime/Shutterstock; page 25: ©Damsea/Shutterstock, ©Ethan Daniels/Shutterstock; page 26: ©banjongseal324SS/Shutterstock, ©xpixel/Shutterstock, ©mastersky/Shutterstock, ©Vladimir Wrangel/Shutterstock; page 27: ©Kamla S/Shutterstock, ©guentermanaus/Shutterstock, ©Petr Toman/Shutterstock; page 28: ©banjongseal324SS/Shutterstock, ©xpixel/Shutterstock, ©guentermanaus/Shutterstock; page 29: ©Francesco_Ricciardi/Shutterstock, ©banjongseal324SS/Shutterstock, ©xpixel/Shutterstock, ©Charlotte Bleijenberg/Shutterstock; page 32: ©banjongseal324SS/Shutterstock

Edited by: Catherine Malaski
Cover and interior layout by: Nick Pearson

Library of Congress PCN Data

Animals That Break the Rules / Natasha Vizcarra
(Nature's Rule Breakers)
ISBN 978-1-73165-802-9 (hard cover)(alk. paper)
ISBN 978-1-73165-808-1 (soft cover)
ISBN 978-1-73165-814-2 (e-book)
ISBN 978-1-73165-820-3 (e-pub)
Library of Congress Control Number: 2024932703

Rourke Educational Media
Printed in the United States of America
01-2222411937